# Bone Scribed

poems || asemics

# Bone Scribed

poems || asemics

Karla Van Vliet

Shanti Arts Publishing

Brunswick, Maine

Bone Scribed: poems || asemics



Published by Shanti Arts Publishing

Interior and cover design by Karla Van Vliet

Cover image: Karla Van Vliet,
*Early Morning Murmur, the Chickadees*

Shanti Arts LLC
193 Hillside Road
Brunswick, Maine 04011
shantiarts.com

Printed in the United States of America

ISBN: 978-1-962082-38-9 (softcover)

There are days when there are not words
for what I must speak.
Those days I must find another way,
for to not speak what needs speaking
is to be a mist lifted off mountain woodlands,
dispersed into the nothingness of sky.

## Other Books by Karla Van Vliet

*She Speaks Tongues: poems || asemic writing*

*Fluency: A Collection of Asemic Writing*

*The River From My Mouth*

*From the Book of Remembrance*

## Chapbooks

*Colors of the Grittiest God,*
a collaboration with Kristine Snodgrass

*Fragments: From the Lost Book of the Bird Spirit*

*Wildwood Devotions: poems || asemics*

# Contents

## Compendium of Notional Words

## Medicine of Blues

# Acknowledgments

The following poems previously appeared in these publications:

*Green Mountains Review Online:* "Compendium of Notional Words"

*The Tishman Review:* "Boat Prayer"

*Green Mountains Review Online:* "The Medicine of Blues"

*Harpy Hybrid Review:* "The Mercy of Two Adjoined"; "From the Crevice of Mercy, Vespers"; "Deep Under Water, So Blue, My Heartbeat"; "Susurrant Voices from Below"; and "Clarity of Blue"

*Habor Review:* "Early Morning Murmur, the Chickadees"

Thank you to the many who support my creative explorations. To my family, my loved ones (you know who you are,) Sue Scavo, Kristine Snodgrass, Liz Powell, Adrie Kusserow, and the amazing asemic community.

I would especially like to thank Christine Cote of Shanti Arts who has, time and again, offered to bring my work into the world. You have been the most gracious conduit, thank you.

# Compendium of Notional Words

::::::::::

gerund

a kind of weeping through the night, the gentle flowing of river water, which has tumbled out of mountain streams to slowly meander along grass lined meadow-banks. It's burbling sounds like those of the mourning dove's cooing and the soft pattering of a light rain, bringing forth longing for the mountain's wildness, and birdsong in the trees, of deer drinking from the brook, and trout jumping pools.

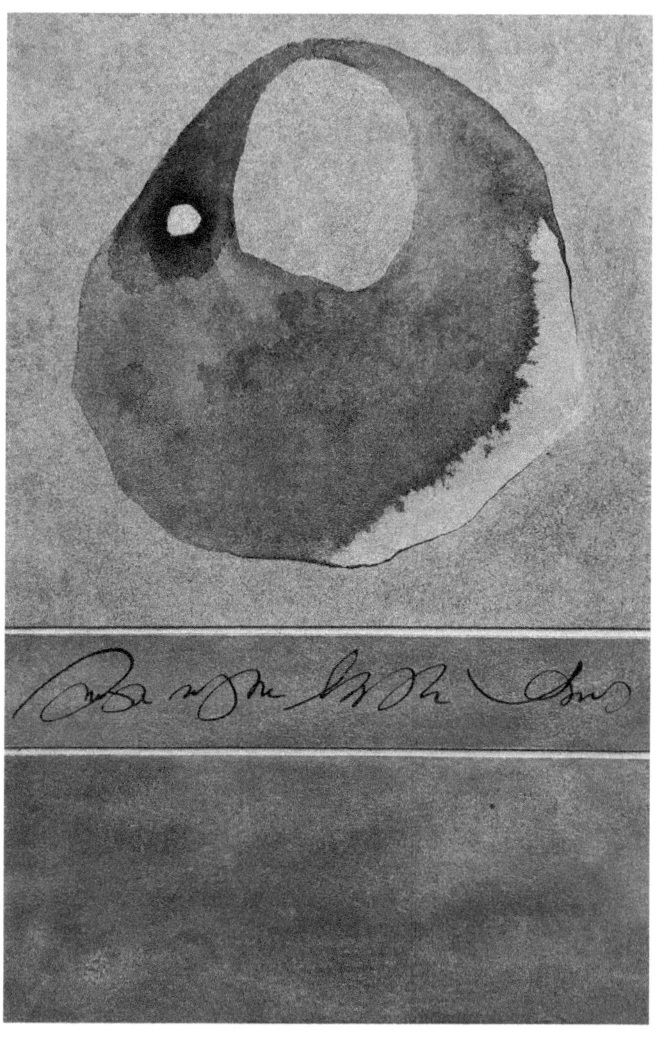

*The Sea's Kindred Solace*

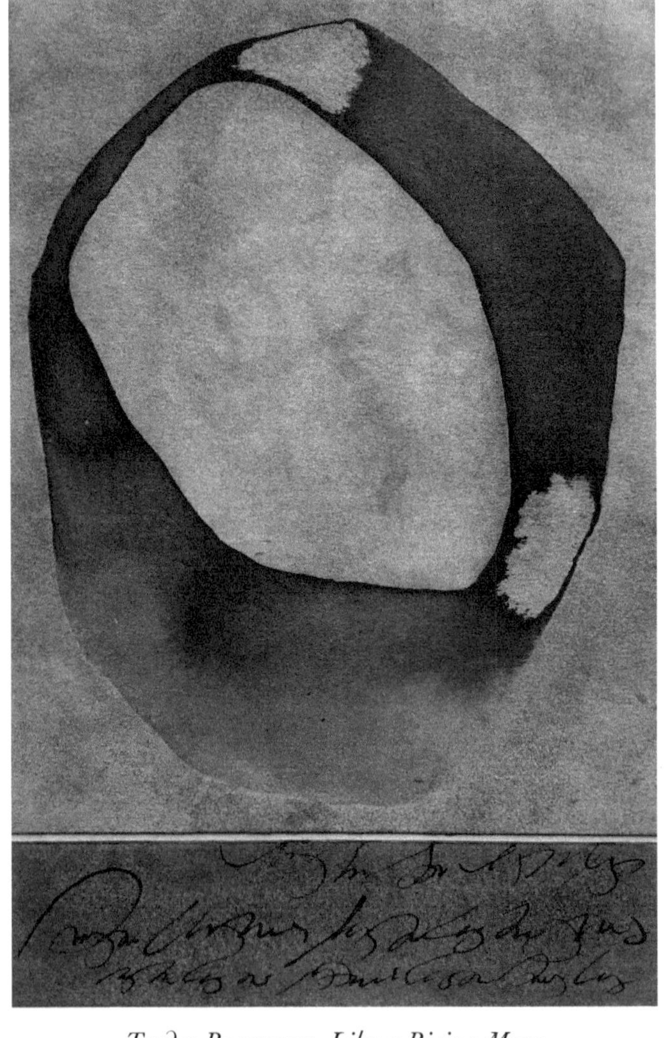

*Tender Resonance, Like a Rising Moon*

:::::::::::

noun

feeling of being shook or struck (as in by lightning) by the presence of another, causing a kind of fundamental change in one's being, an awareness that one now stands on new ground. Often accompanied with a sense of disquiet, not knowing the consequences of such shifting, a rustling of dry leaves coming from just under the rock outcrop, from the bear's den, in early spring.

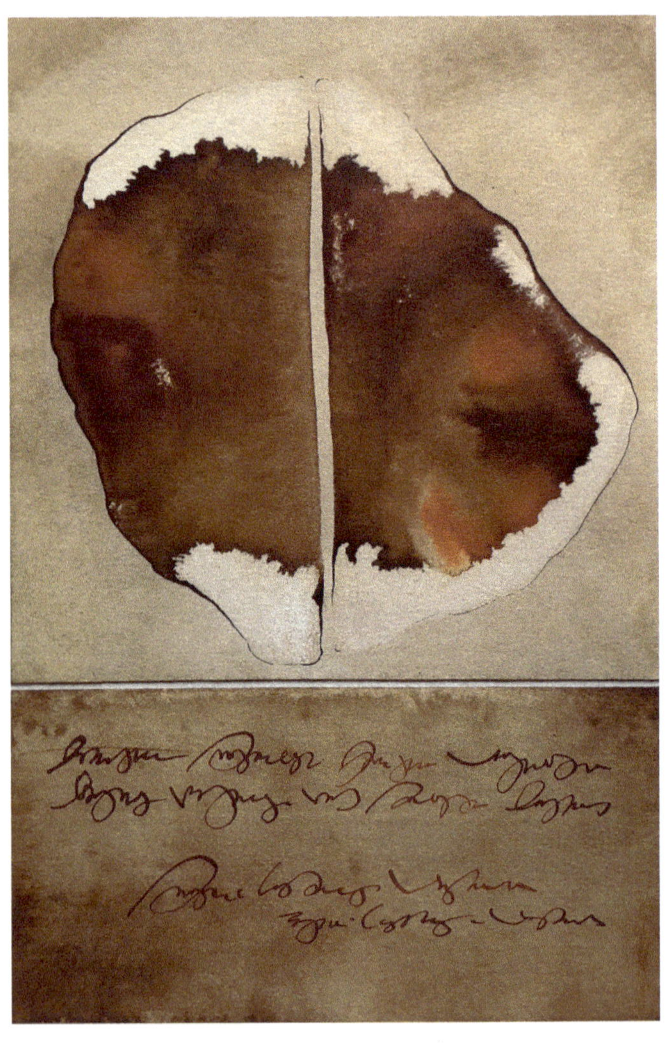

*The Seed's First Rumbling*

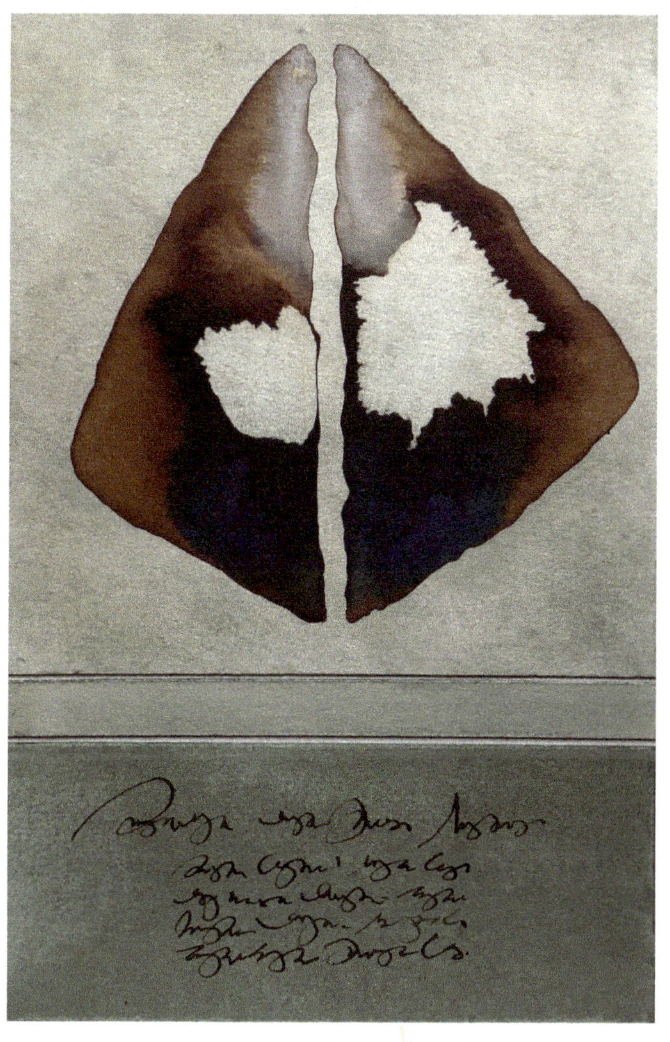

*The Mercy of Two Adjoined*

:::::::

noun

a kind of love that conveys the sense of having known the beloved from before recognized time; where the feelings of love are attributed to the continued blossoming of hardy lilac shrubs and ancient apple trees, often located on untended homesteads at the end of long unkempt dirt roads within wooded areas that nature has reclaimed.

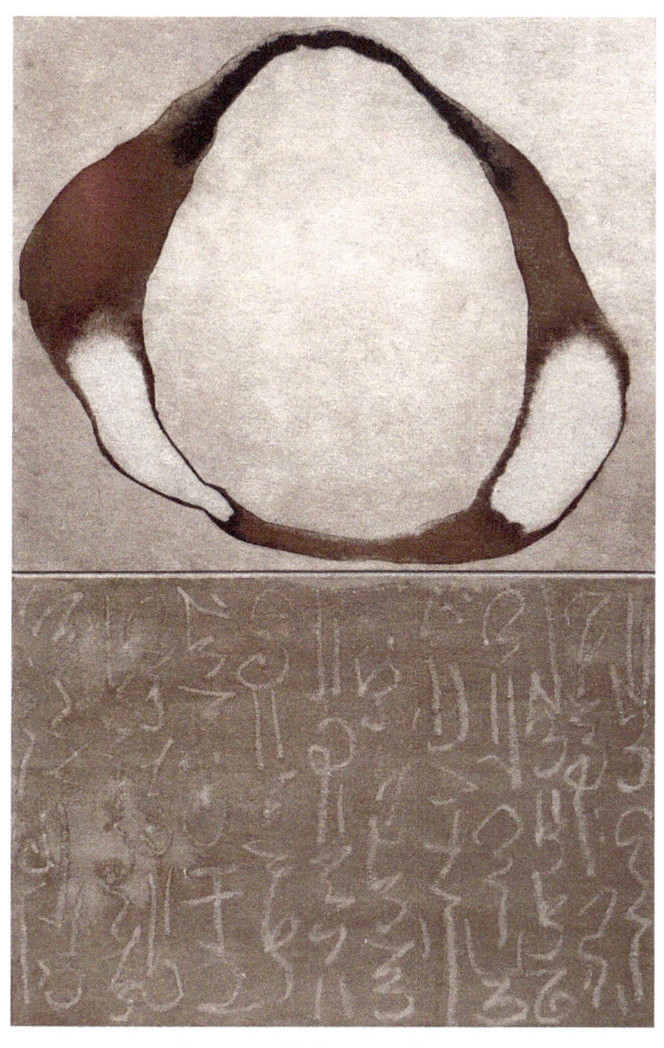

*Vespers, Wind Swept Horizon*

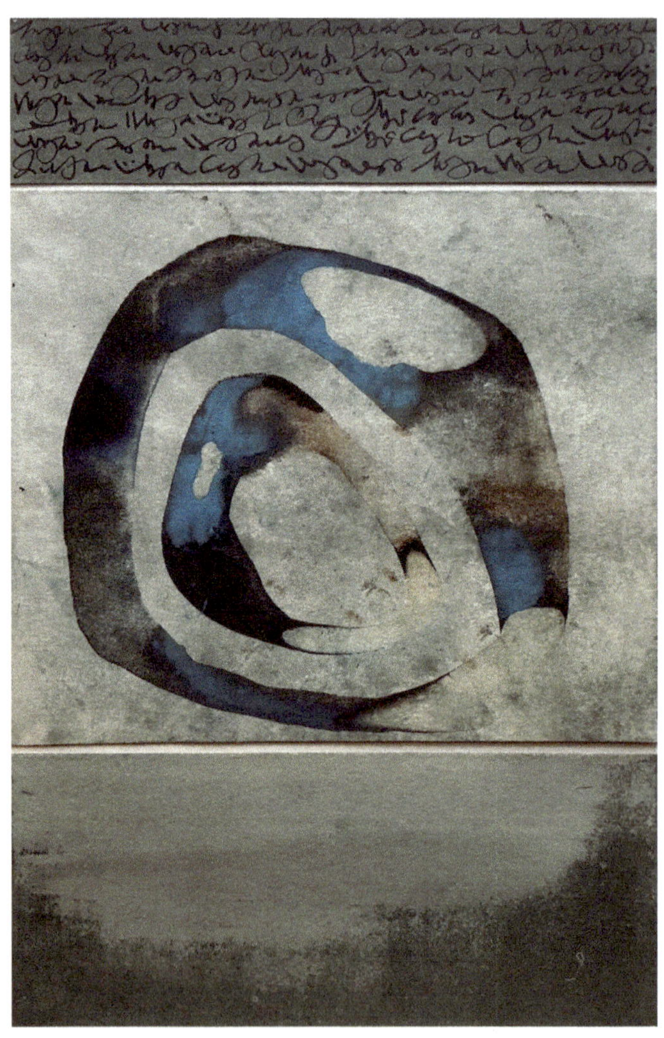

*Reverberation, The Mourning Dove's Morning Coo*

:::::::::::::

verb

the act of coming up behind another causing the other to feel, simultaneously, the sensation of easing into the warmth of a hot spring, a resting place enclosed by frosted greenery discovered while walking through the mountains in cold winter, and the sense of lifting into the sky as a flock of pigeons from a rooftop, wings slapping the air so as to make a whooshing sound, and to momentarily disappear in a tight turn of flight.

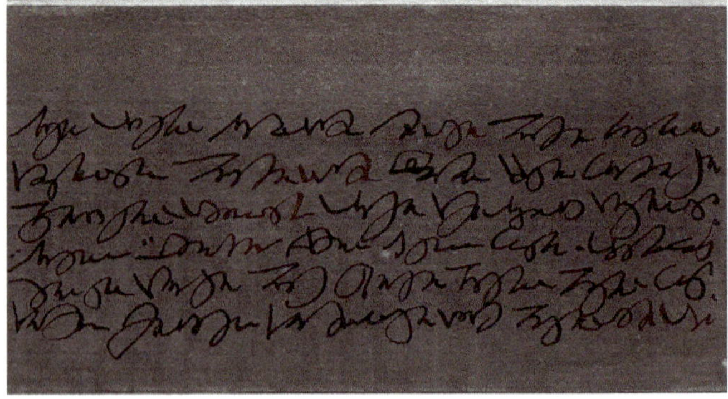

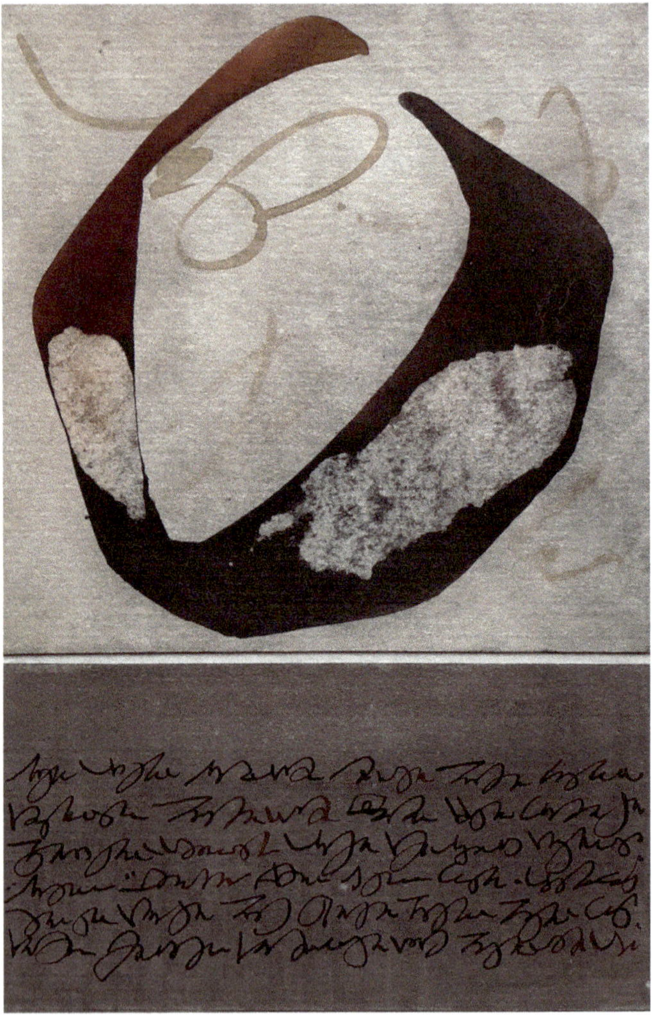

*Early Morning Murmur, The Chickadees*

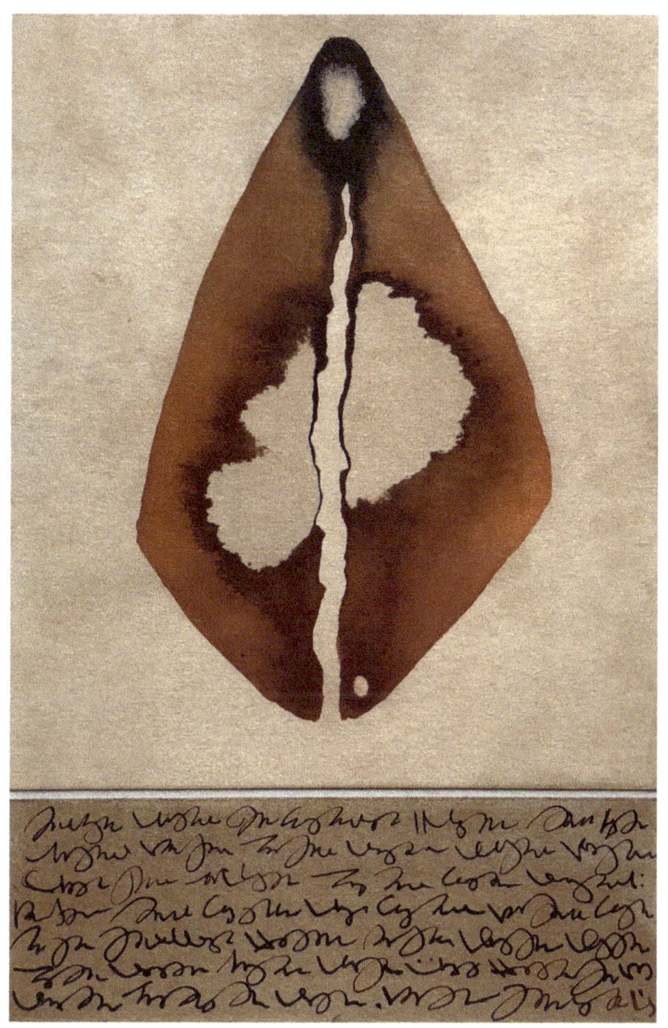

*From the Crevice of Mercy, Vespers*

:::::::::

noun

the inability to remove a person from one's thoughts, most often accompanied by a kind of vibration in the chest similar to the flickering light of fireflies over a summer meadow or minnows in a shallow pool; their silver dartings.

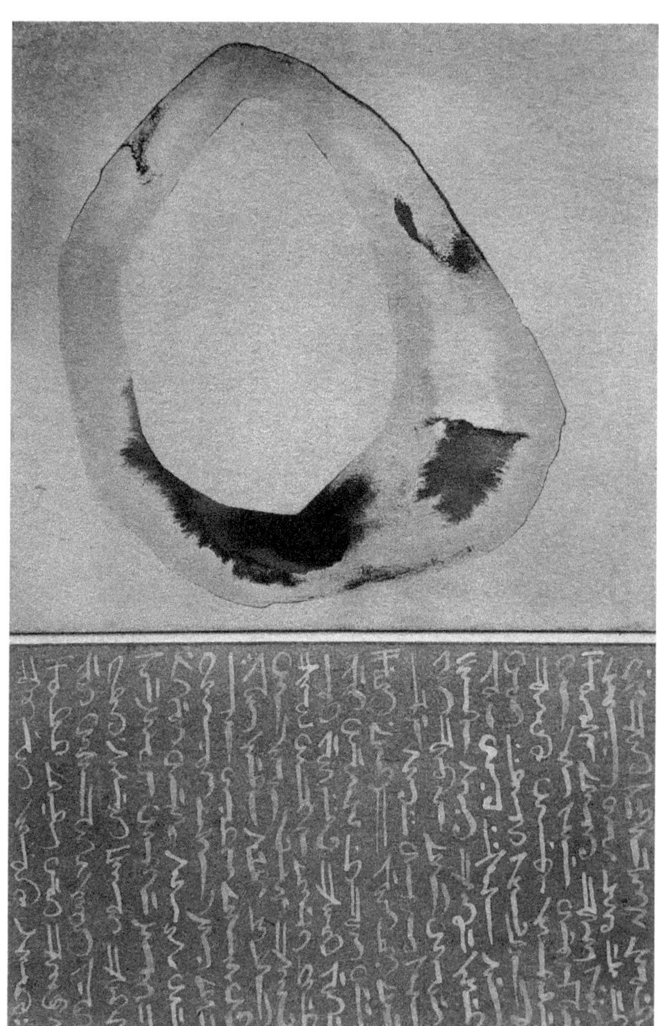

*Cold Dawn Calls Out to the Frozen River*

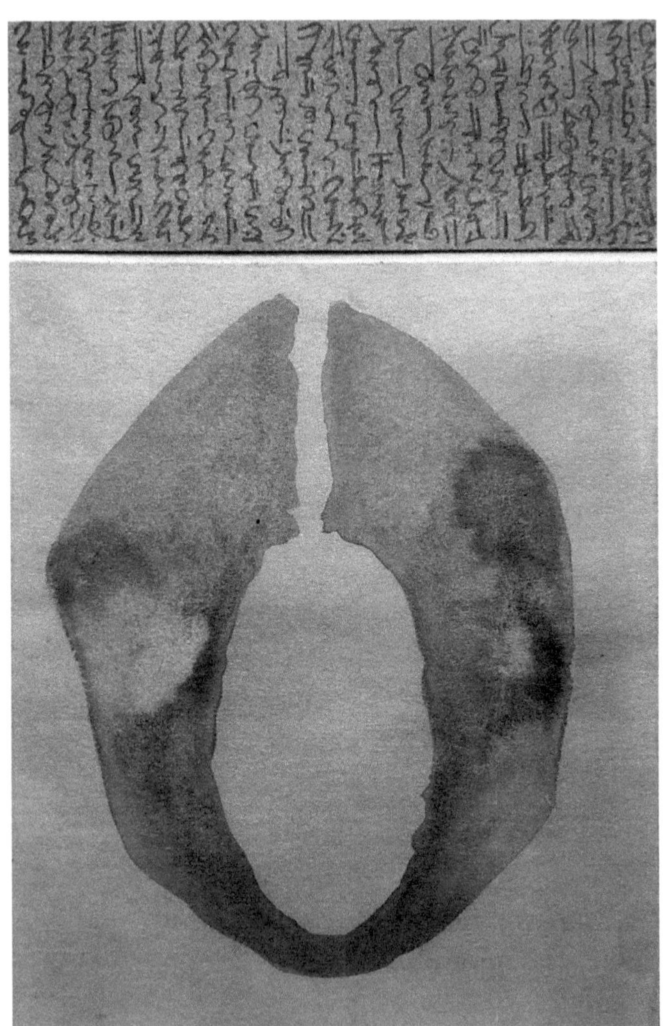

*The Sea's Cadence, A Boat Grace Longed For*

## Boat Prayer

I.

I hold my hands in the shape of a boat to deliver
this prayer.

II.

Like a flower, my hands the innermost petals,
the prayer my own heart.

III.

The moon-slip in this dusk sky, hands, a boat
in darkness.

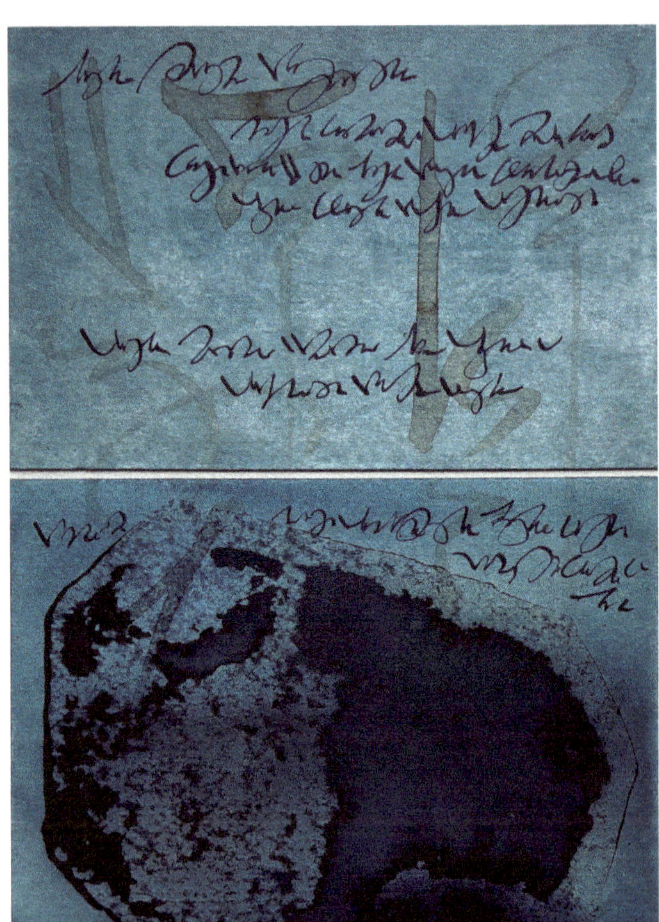

*Deep Under Water, So Blue, My Heartbeat*

# Medicine of Blues

*Indigo:*

dusk enters me / inside I am night / I am dream / the hills are crow filled / a man touches my hand / no, before that, his voice like bird flight / a Japanese poem / an unraveling in wind / enters like ink / now, his hand on my hand / the lustrous wings rustle / my heart beats dye stained text / mountain reaches toward sky / moon reflects on water / a plum / blossom of fallen snow / this dawn rising

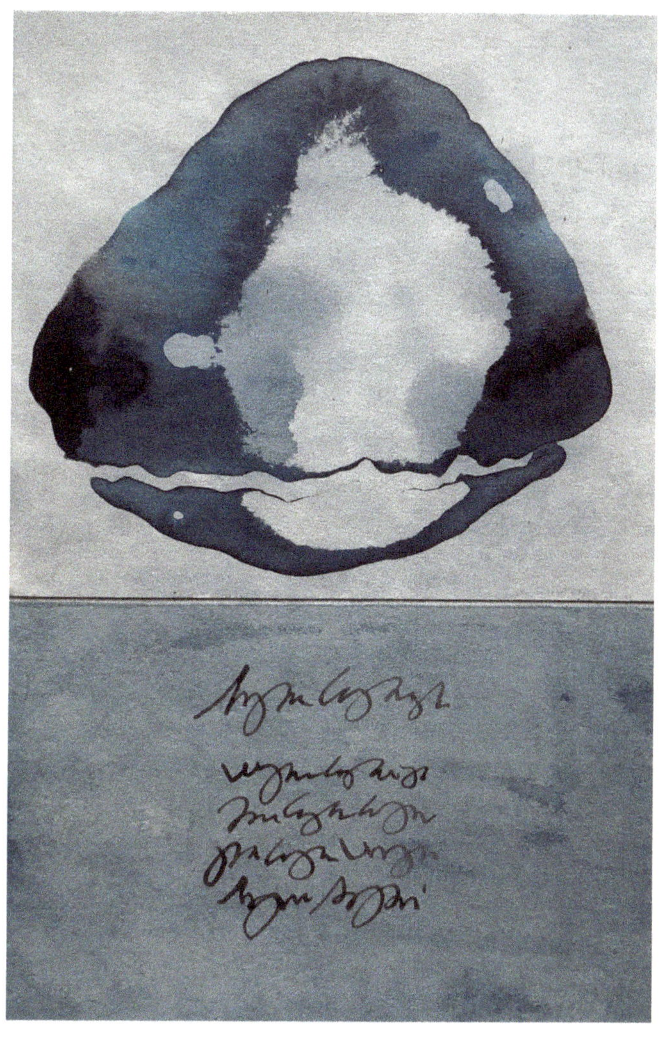

*Spring Pond Serenade*

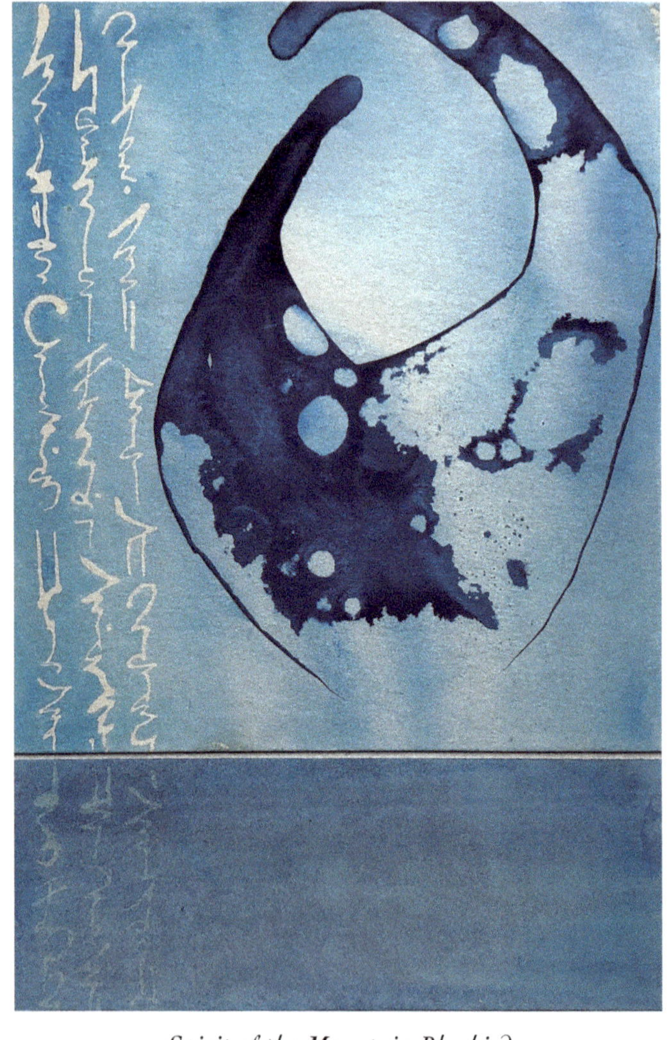

*Spirit of the Mountain Bluebird*

*Cerulean:*

I swallow sky / blue vault strewn with bird / so far the horizon / thin calligraphy of mountains / between here and there / I am song / or soaring / a boundless surge of script / these crane bodies flying / his voice's tenor / rustling flight / I am riding the poem's thermals / a snow field melts / intimate mist holds close / blooming orchid's fragile grace

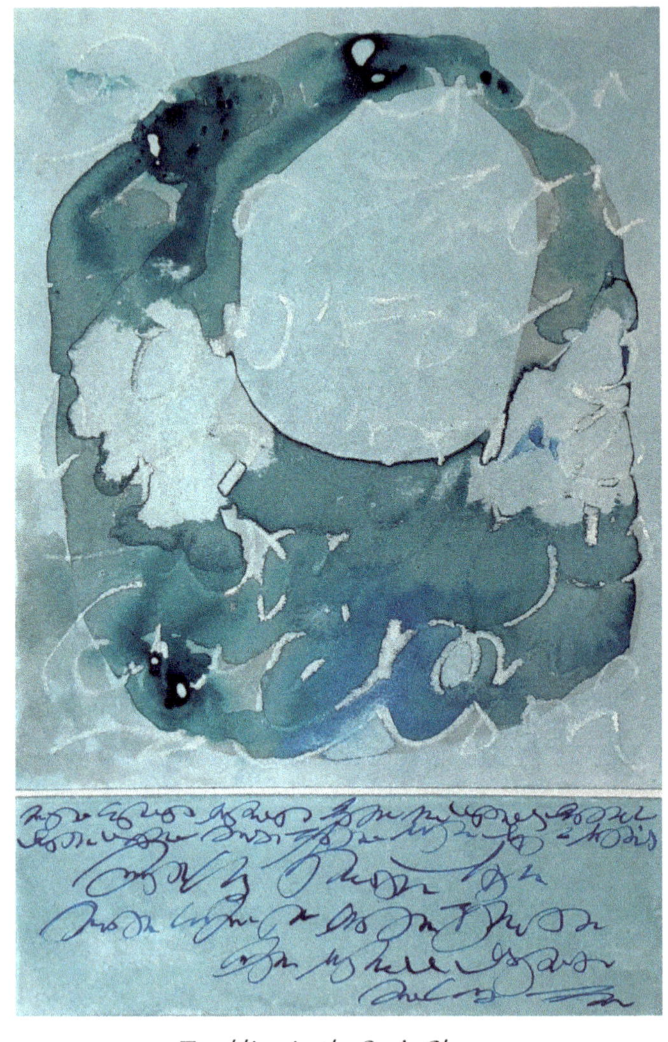

*Tumbling in the Sea's Clamor*

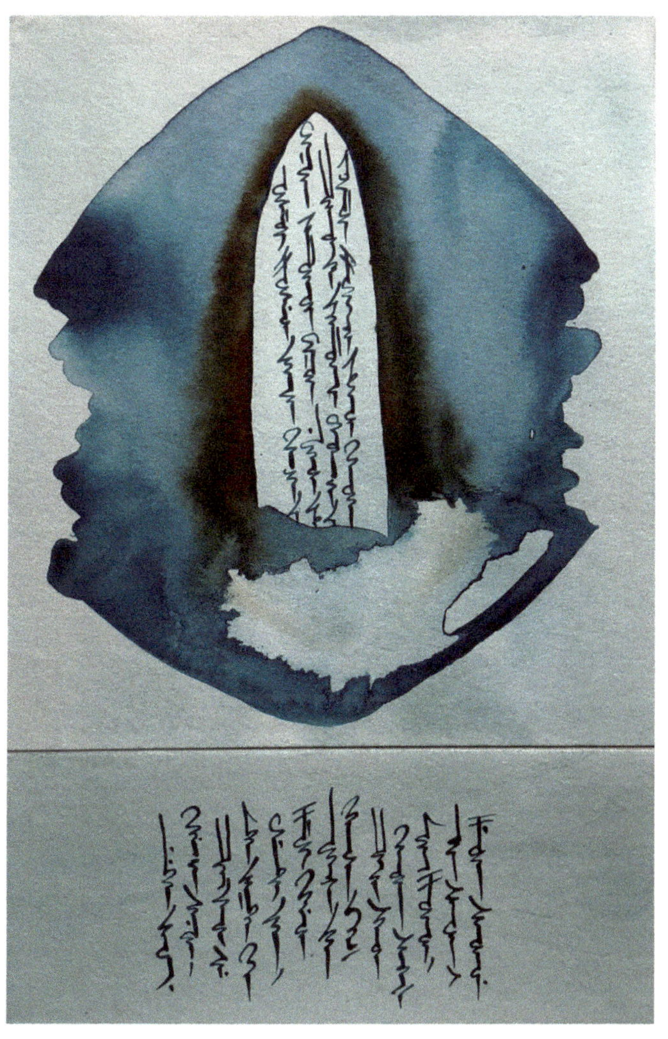

*Dawn's Cerulean Testimony*

*Turquoise:*

scavenge blue stone / in my hand, sky / rainfall / earth and heavens joined / poem carving into me a long river / peacock's plume / bird's cry / I have been so thirsty / the desert ground / cracked vessel / his voice a soaking inscription / dormant seed sprout / grasses, a lyrical fan / the wind like fingers caressing my face / a silk curtain / a thousand petals / the scent of wet clay

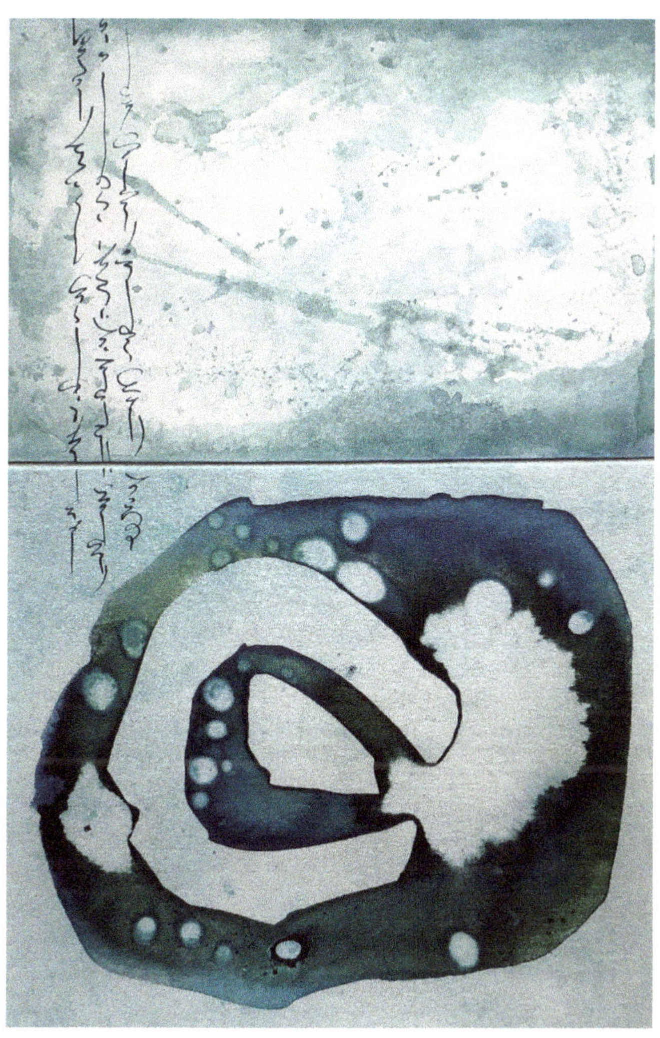

*In the Thawing*

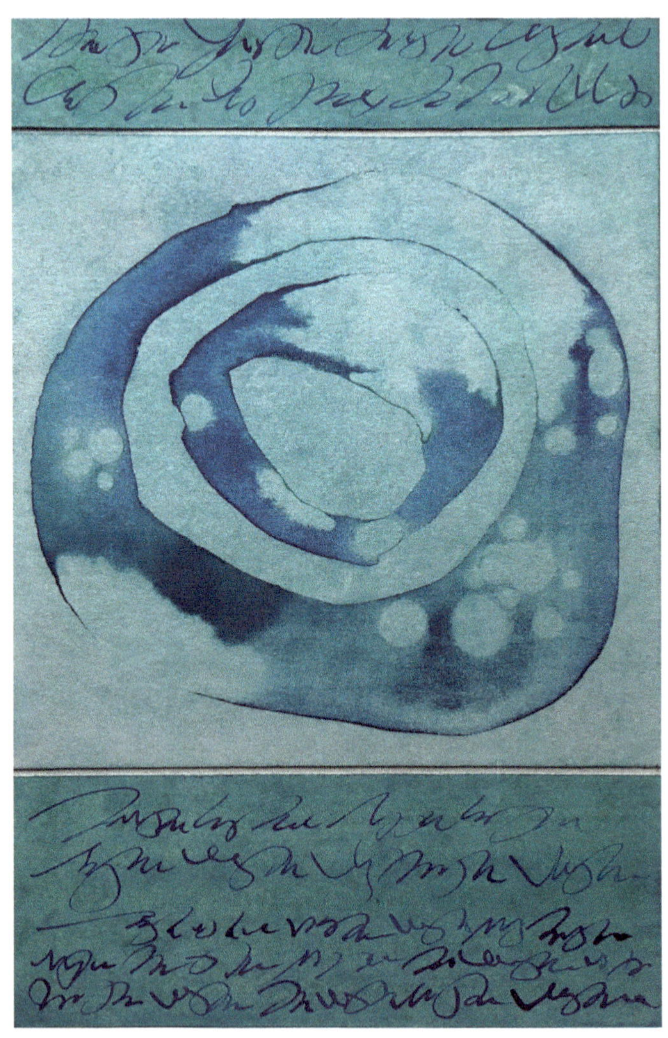

*Song of the Underwater*

*Aquamarine:*

I sing rain-showers / my tongue a deep sea / each word a wing against wind / swan flight / lifting white beacon / his hand in mine / belonging lives on the edge of kindness / a scroll unwound / path through the mountains / lingering mist / fluted brook / the blue-green light of a bamboo forest / fingers intertwined / roots / the feathered moon lands amongst the reeds / sails forth

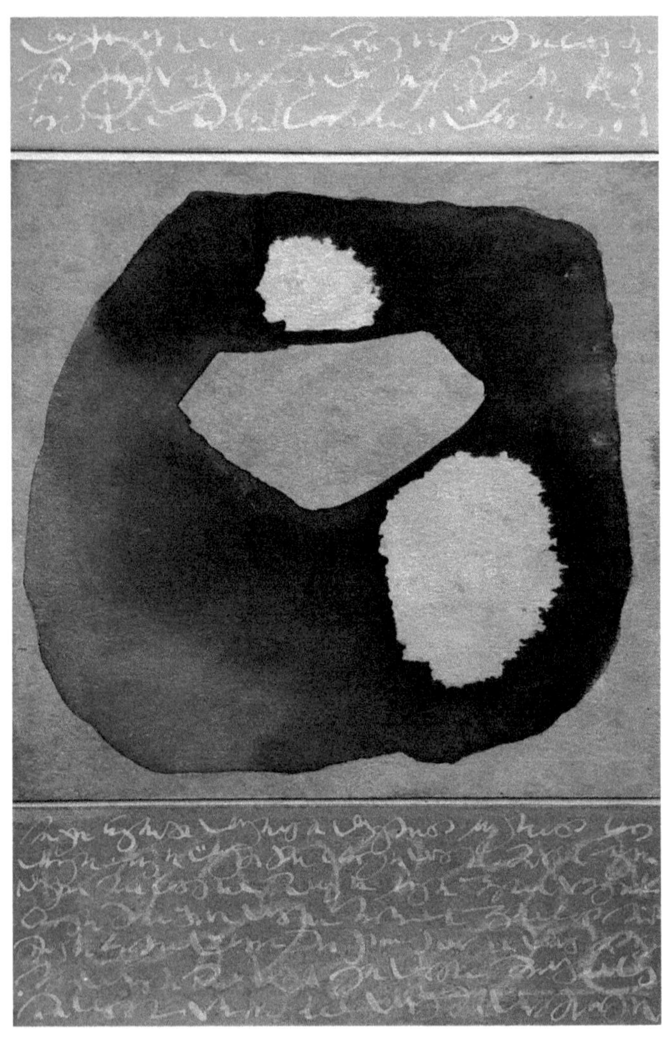

*Susurrant Voices from Below*

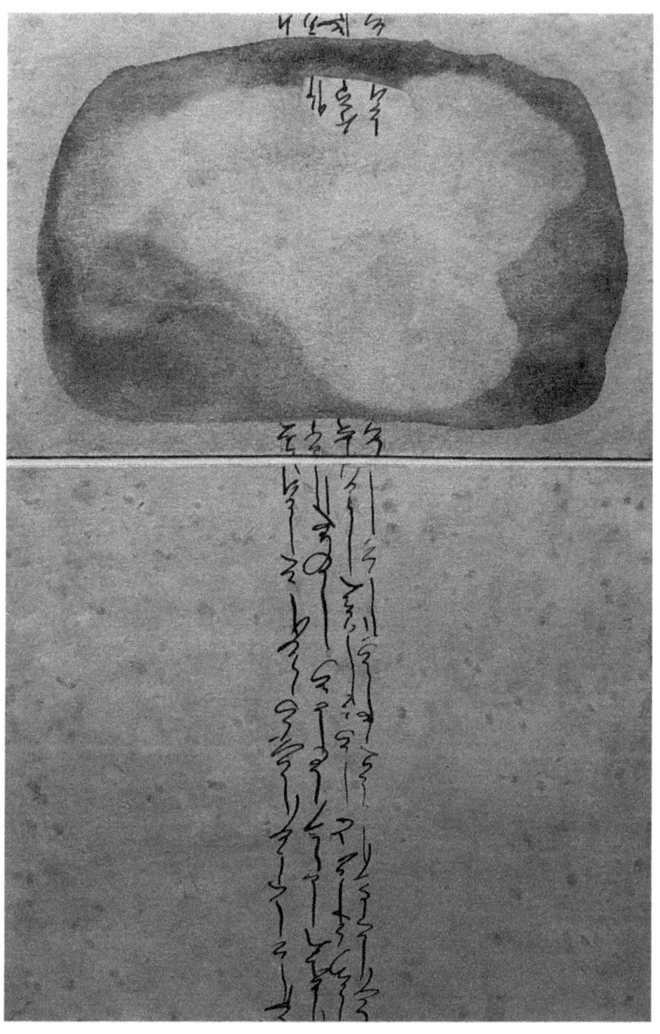

*Invocation of the Misty Hillside*

*Luminous:*

ball of blue light / in my dream, a gift / his love inscribed like tenderness / cipher / noon sky / flocked buntings splinter like sunbeams / bone light / to take his hand / flying white winged across rice paper / cinnabar sealed / the heart noted in the lucent body / beating / call from the mountain temple / scattered fireflies in the valley / shimmering assertion / his shoulder to rest my head / to rest

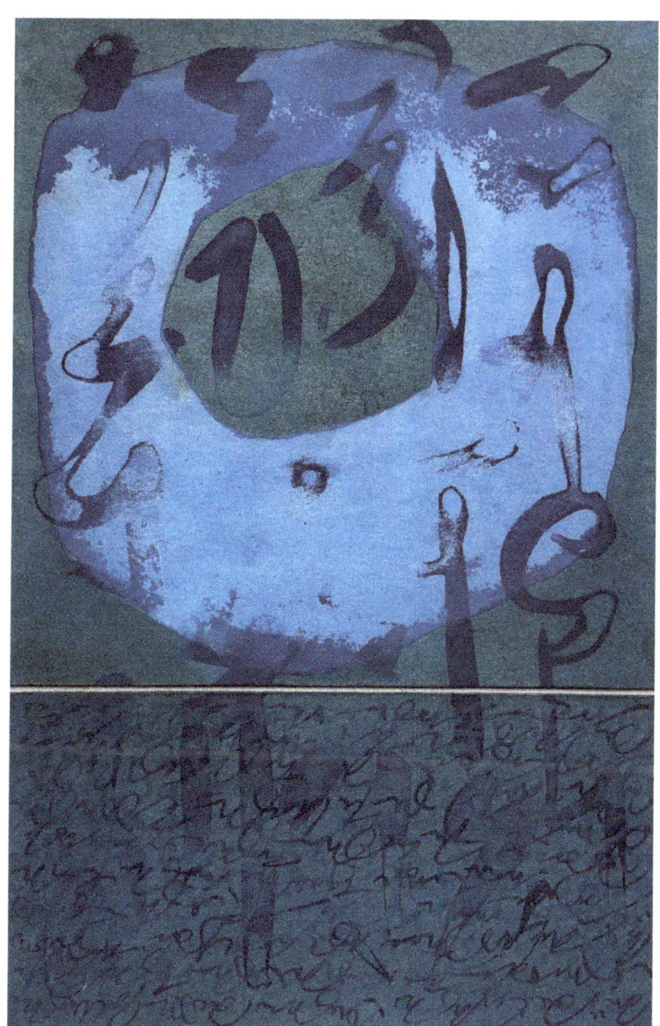

*Clarity of Blue*

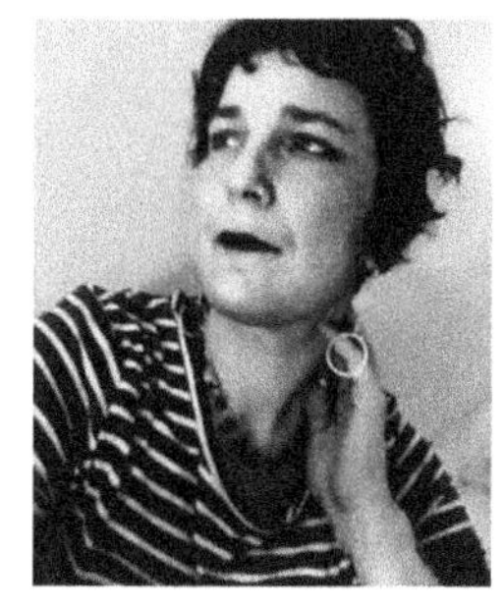

**Karla Van Vliet** is an artist, writer, gallerist, and dream-analyst. She is the author of eight collections. Her poems, asemics, and artwork have appeared worldwide. Karla is co-founder and editor of *∂eLuge Journa*l and the founder of Van Vliet Gallery, which showcases art and asemics from around the world. For more information visit vanvlietarts.com.

# Shanti Arts

Nature • Art • Spirit

Please visit us online
to browse our entire book catalog,
including poetry collections and fiction,
books on travel, nature, healing, art,
photography, and more.

Also take a look at our highly regarded art
and literary journal, *Still Point Arts Quarterly*,
which may be downloaded for free.

www.shantiarts.com

www.ingramcontent.com/pod-product-compliance
Lightning Source LLC
LaVergne TN
LVHW052357100826
845147LV00013B/863

* 9 7 8 1 9 6 2 0 8 2 3 8 9 *